# FROM LAB TO MARKET
The Process of Commercializing Medical Technologies

# FROM LAB TO MARKET
## The Process of Commercializing Medical Technologies

**AUTHOR**
Elias Caro

**CONTRIBUTORS**
Manuel Kingsley
Brian Walsh

**EDITOR**
D'Lynne Plummer

**DESIGNER**
Jim Densmore

**Biocomx.org**

Copyright © 2018 by Elias Caro
All rights reserved. This book or any portion thereof
may not be reproduced or used in any manner whatsoever
without the express written permission of the publisher
except for the use of brief quotations in a book review.
Printed in the United States of America
First Printing, 2018
ISBN: 9781791382605

Dedicated to Sue Van,

President and CEO of the Wallace H. Coulter Foundation, whose vision inspired us to make training university innovators our mission.

And, to Wallace H. Coulter,

the benefactor who inspired all who knew him to pursue the dream of a better world in which Science Serves Humanity.

| | |
|---|---|
| **SECTION ONE: VALIDATING THE PROBLEM** | 4 |
| 1.1 Cycle of Care: Understanding the Patient Journey | 5 |
| 1.2 User Interviews | 8 |
| **SECTION TWO: YOUR VALUE PROPOSITION** | 10 |
| **SECTION THREE: BUSINESS CASE VALIDATION** | 15 |
| 3.1 Market Size | 16 |
| 3.2 Who Will Pay? | 19 |
| 3.3 Other Models | 20 |
| 3.4 The Shift to Value-Based Health care | 20 |
| 3.5 Pricing Strategy | 21 |
| 3.6 Your Financial Model | 24 |
| **SECTION FOUR: UNDERSTANDING INVESTMENT AND FINANCING** | 25 |
| 4.1 Non-Dilutive Financing | 26 |
| 4.2 Dilutive Financing | 27 |
| **SECTION 5: BRINGING IT ALL TOGETHER—YOUR BUSINESS MODEL** | 28 |
| **SECTION 6: COMMERCIALIZATION: AN EXERCISE IN DE-RISKING** | 30 |
| 6.1 FDA Medical Device Regulatory Classifications | 31 |
| 6.2 Reimbursement | 34 |
| 6.3 Intellectual Property (IP) | 35 |
| 6.4 Technology Validation | 37 |
| 6.5 Market Risk | 38 |
| 6.6 Scale-Up Manufacturing | 39 |
| 6.7 Management Team | 40 |
| 6.8 Valuation and Funding | 41 |
| **SECTION 7: CASE STUDIES** | 46 |
| **APPENDIX** | 53 |

# PREFACE

This guide is written for biomedical innovators seeking to improve the lives of patients by translating innovative technologies into medical technologies. The contents are focused primarily on business principles that have been distilled from hundreds of projects as part of the Coulter Foundation's **Translational Partners Program** and **Coulter Translational Reward Awards.** To date, the Foundation has funded more than 600 projects, which in the first 11 years have raised close to $6 billion in funding.

The course **Concept to Clinic: Commercializing Innovation (C3i),** offered by the National Institutes of Health (NIH), forms the basis of this Guide. This course has helped hundreds of university innovators, engineers, clinicians, and scientists learn how to commercialize the technologies they have developed in a very demanding market. The C3i program is based on the Coulter commercialization process, an approach to biomedical research translation developed and continuously refined by the Foundation in collaboration with its academic partners across the country.

We want to thank all the individuals who have helped university innovators pursue the long and highly regulated paths to bring medical products to market and from whom we have distilled insights to produce this guide. In particular we want to recognize:

David Chen, Cierra Crowder, Frank Debernardis, Andrew Dimeo, Steve Fening, Rachael Hagan, Shahram Hejazi, Cynthia Helphingstine, Tuan Hoang, Kathie Jordan, Manuel Kingsley, Shawna Khouri, Thomas Marten, Christine Matheson, Robert Morff, Barry Myers, Mara Neal, Mark Nikolsky, Andrea Nye, Rifat Pamukcu, Grace Powers, Kathy Reuther, Gordon Saul, Donna See, Stephen Snowdy, John Schneider, Kassandra Thomson, Brian Walsh, Lisa Waples, Paul Yock, and others who have been invaluable partners in this project.

As part of this guide, we have assembled a video library for your reference. In this library you will find videos and presentations related to each section of this course and guide.

To view these resources at any time, go to **www.biocomx.org/FLTM** and enter the password **c3i$Fltm**.

# INTRODUCTION

Successful medical innovations present a solution to a problem. New drugs, diagnostic methods, drug delivery systems, and medical devices offer the hope of better treatment and of care that is less costly, disruptive, and painful. If you have identified an unmet need—and invented a means to solve it—you may be wondering how to successfully translate your biomedical technology from lab to market.

**Part I** of this guide is designed to help you approach this challenge by summarizing the steps to commercializing your product. It focuses on validating your solution in the context of the marketplace, including understanding the patient journey and identifying stakeholders, as well as determining whether there is a viable financial opportunity to bring your product[1] to market.

**Part II** of this guide focuses on mitigating the risks of bringing innovations to market, from regulatory requirements and reimbursement to intellectual property, valuation and funding, and management issues.

[1] We use the word "product" as a generalization to indicate any medical device, diagnostic test, drug or procedure.

# SECTION 1
# VALIDATING THE PROBLEM

No matter how confident you are in your product idea, you must be able to prove the problem is a real one that needs solving. Validating the problem requires you to answer the following key questions:

> **?** How is the problem currently addressed or solved?

> **?** Who would be positively or negatively impacted if my product were implemented?

To answer these questions, you must endeavor to better understand the patient journey as it relates to the problem.

## 1.1 CYCLE OF CARE: UNDERSTANDING THE PATIENT JOURNEY

In all industries and for all products, empathizing with the needs of target consumers is an essential step in product design and validation. It is important to gather as much data about the users, their needs, and the problems that underlie the development of that particular product.

In the health care context, disease-based care cycles are a useful tool for properly understanding the status of the care process for a given medical condition, often revealing how to improve cost effectiveness, access, and quality of care. In conjunction with quality improvement studies, they can show the strengths and weaknesses within the health care continuum.[2] These visual maps capture all phases of an episode that correspond to its progression from outset to closing.

Journey mapping begins with a baselining step intended to capture the current patient experience (irrelevant of your product) from multiple perspectives, as well as interactions within the clinical environment. At each phase, the patient and relevant providers share various touchpoints—action and information flows between people, devices, and systems. The resulting visualization helps to identify inter- and cross-organizational gaps in areas such as data flow, compliance, availability of relevant information, etc.

Perhaps most importantly, this exercise also helps to identify relevant stakeholders. A stakeholder is any medical personnel, institution, regulatory agency, investor, medical company, or patient group interested in the effect or outcome of the adoption of a new medical product. Each type of stakeholder can impact the success of a new product.

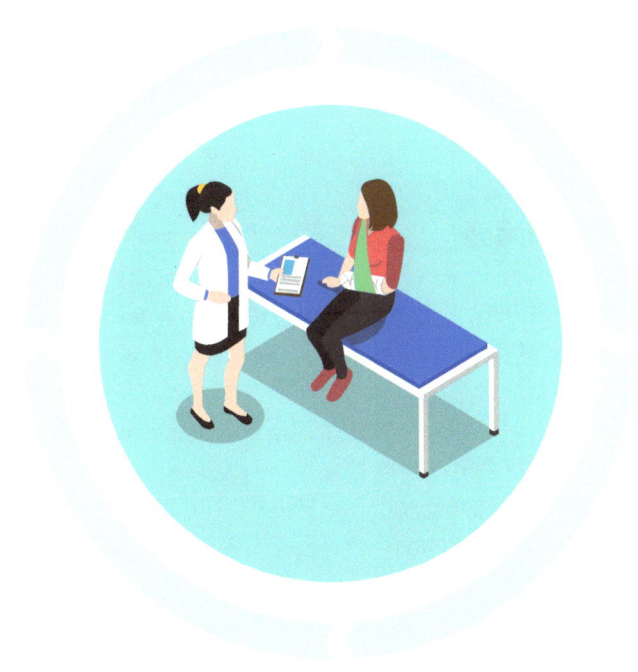

[2] Verbeek XAAM, Lord WP. *The Care Cycle: An Overview*. Medicamundi, 2007

**To better understand how this exercise works, let's map the care continuum that a patient follows after experiencing a heart rhythm anomaly:**

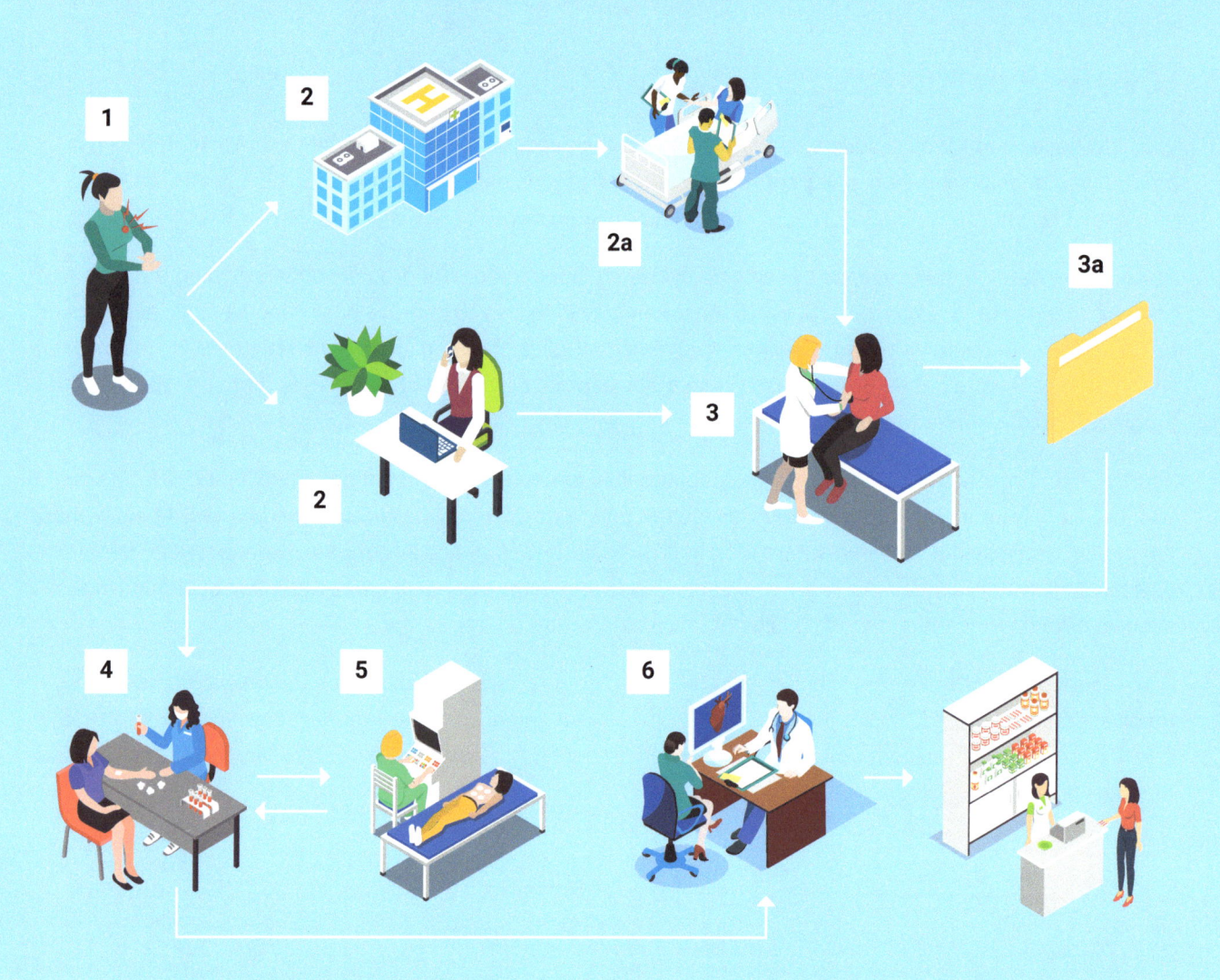

**Step 1** The patient has an arrhythmia episode.

**Step 2** She can either make an appointment with her doctor or go to an emergency department (ED) or walk-in clinic (WC).

**Step 2a** She can be released from the ED or WC or be hospitalized. In either case, after stabilization, she will be referred for an appointment with her primary care physician (PCP).

**Step 3** The patient sees her PCP, who performs an electrocardiogram (ECG) and may request blood work and cardiac monitor.

**Step 3a** Depending on test results from the PCP and the ED/WC, the PCP may initiate treatment and refer the patient to a cardiologist.

**Step 4** The cardiologist typically runs some tests in the office and requests additional tests.

**Step 5** The tests are performed by the appropriate specialty.

**Step 6** The cardiologist discusses the results with the patient and recommends a course of action.

1.1 CYCLE OF CARE: UNDERSTANDING THE PATIENT JOURNEY

Continuing with this heart rhythm anomaly hypothetical, let's assume your product is a wearable patch that can record a continuous ECG for 15 days. At the end of the 15 days, the patch is read by a machine. This product competes with the short-term cardiac monitor and the long-term cardiac monitor.

The cycle of care diagram we have mapped above identifies several influencers and potential stakeholders for your product, including:

**The PCP, who can introduce the product to the patient**

**The cardiologist, who can decide between a long-term cardiac monitor and the patch**

Note that if the patient has an HMO, there could be a restriction on the patch, as it may be more expensive than a cardiac monitor that the HMO has already purchased. Most hospitals have a committee that evaluates technologies and decides which ones will be approved. In the committee there may be medical personnel who oppose the patch due to economic or technical reasons.

As a part of this exercise, it is important to understand how your new product will integrate in the users' practice and workflow—or if your product changes the users altogether. A new product might displace a procedure—and the associated revenue—from one discipline or service to another. For example, a virtual colonoscopy moves revenue from gastroenterology to radiology. The machine learning capabilities of IBM Watson may reduce or eliminate the need of radiologists and pathologists for routine diagnostic work. It is more than likely that the displaced disciplines will oppose the change, so it's important to bear this in mind from the start.

Once the optimum level of granularity for your product's cycle of care has been mapped, you will have a clear understanding of the types of clinical personnel you must talk to in order to validate whether the problem you are planning to tackle is of high importance—in other words, if solved or improved, it would change medical practice. Keep in mind that you may need to interview different clinical specialties. You may also need to interview several clinicians inside the same specialty who recommend different treatment avenues related to your identified problem.

## 1.2. USER INTERVIEWS

Just as empathizing with the patient is an important aspect of validating the problem, so too is exploring the perspectives of users and other stakeholders, such as medical personnel and clinicians, who will be affected by or play a role in the use of your product. Focus group and stakeholder interviews are qualitative methods that elicit open-ended responses and allow respondents to describe their needs/pain points/experience in their own words.

Focus groups typically take place in-person (although other formats, such as online groups are common). Personal interviews may take place either face to face (preferred), by video conference, or over the telephone. Both approaches typically use an interview guide (a set of predetermined questions) to keep the conversation on track and ensure consistency across the interviews.

We highly suggest individual interviews over focus groups, as strong personalities tend to dominate that latter. This makes independent opinions difficult to obtain from more reserved or thoughtful participants, especially in the absence of experienced facilitators.

Interview guides have a few basic components:

- **Qualifying questions:** These questions help ensure you are talking to the right clinician. Make sure experience, training, patient focus, and volume is appropriate.

- **General questions:** Establish common ground on the problem you are trying to address.

- **Specific probing questions:** Dig deeper into specific aspects of the problem, use setting, limitations, or important aspects for product design.

[3] Use caution when sharing information about your products. Make sure your IP is filed, and keep your discussion generic.

---

### Sample Interview Guide Questions

These sample questions are extracted from an interview guide for catheter design inputs. The goal of the stakeholder interviews for this product is to better understand the selection criteria for catheters used in endovascular procedures—more specifically, the challenges and limitations associated with more complex procedures. The complete sample interview guide can be found in the appendix

**Qualifying Questions**
- What is your specialty?
- What is your monthly procedure volume?
- What are the most common procedures you perform?
- What are the highest complexity procedures you perform.

**General Questions**
- As we understand it, there are different brands and types of catheters used in endovascular procedures. Do you typically start all procedures with the same catheter?
- What is your monthly procedure volume?
- Which brands(s) do you typically use?
- Are there particular ones that you use less frequently? Specialty? For which use?

**Specific/Probing Questions**
- What determines the specific catheter that you select for a given task?
- Does the specific procedure impact the initial catheter selection? How so?
- What are some of the important attributes when considering steerable catheters? Stiffness on the back end of the catheters? Ability to grip? Tip properties?

**Open-Ended Questions**
- Are there particular procedures for which a product like the one we described might be useful?
- Are there specific concerns that come to mind?
- What would it take to convince you to try/adopt a new steerable catheter?

- **Open-ended queries:** Give your interviewee the opportunity to make comments, express concerns, or surface other relevant points. If you choose to share a description of your product, you may also ask open-ended questions related to your innovation to learn what advantages or disadvantages they might foresee of if any concerns come to mind.

As part of your question set, ask stakeholders to indicate the five problems that, if solved, would have the greatest impact on their practice. Try to explore issues related to workflow, level of difficulty, patient outcomes, and time to perform.[4]

In this stage of the interview, do not talk about your technology; keep the discussion oriented on the problem. Try to understand each of the problems that the user considers important—these unmet needs may become the basis of subsequent or related projects. Once you have understood the problems that they have indicated, you can then bring your problem to the discussion. If this was not one of the problems they named, try to learn why they don't consider it sufficiently important.

## Pressure-Testing Your Hypothesis

While resources and funding can be replaced, you can never get back the time invested in a project that won't succeed. The goal of these interviews is to pressure-test your hypothesis. It is better to know sooner rather than later if your project is bound to fail, so that you can move on to more promising opportunities.

If the users with whom you meet identify your hypothesis as a valid problem, you may discuss the attributes of your solution.[5] Special emphasis should be placed on understanding the deficiencies and virtues of the product they use now. Throughout the interview, be sure to ask open-ended questions rather than yes/no or leading questions. For example, if you ask a clinician, "Do you think a therapy that reduces prostate brachytherapy complications is necessary?" he or she will likely provide a yes or no answer and may assume this is the focus of your project.

---

[4] Note that decreasing procedure time only adds value for the provider if there is a significant demand for the procedure and your product saves enough time to allow the practitioner to perform an additional procedure in its entirety.

[5] Focus on the product attributes and not the design, so as to protect your innovation and keep the conversation more open ended.

# SECTION 2

# YOUR VALUE PROPOSITION

A value proposition refers to a business or marketing statement that a company uses to summarize why a stakeholder should buy a product or use a service. A value proposition explains what benefit your product provides for each stakeholder, and why it is distinctly better than the alternatives.

We will cover four steps to creating a compelling value proposition:[1]

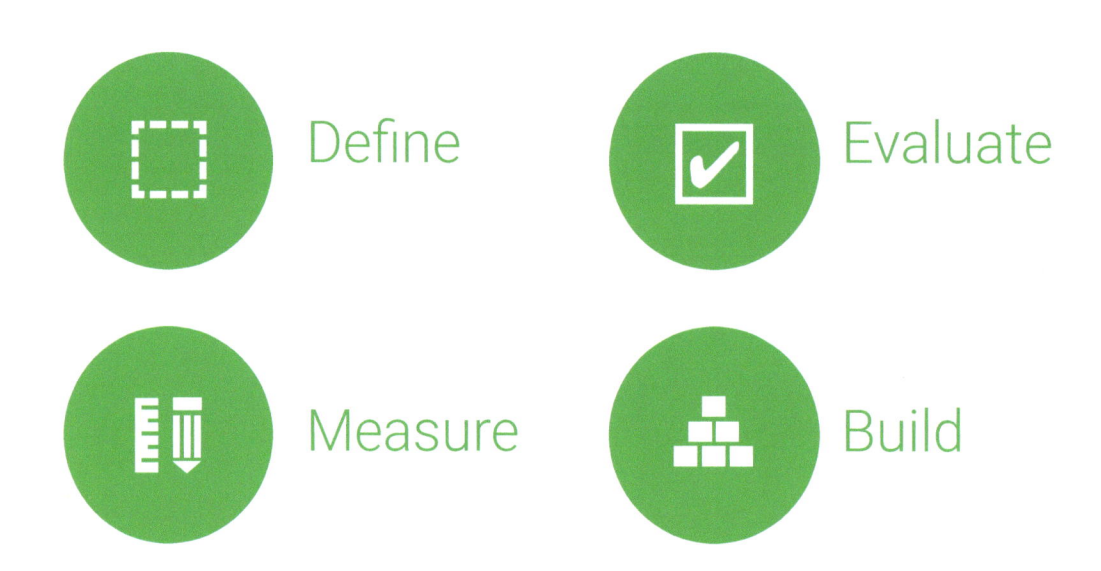

- Define
- Evaluate
- Measure
- Build

[1] https://www.forbes.com/sites/michaelskok/2013/06/14/4-steps-to-building-a-compelling-value-proposition/

# Define

In Section One, we set out to validate that the problem you are trying to solve is critical and required. Does your solution fix a broken business process where there are real, measurable consequences to inaction? Is the market seemingly absent of valid solutions to this problem? As a result of your user interviews, you should have a better sense of whether your solution is a priority.

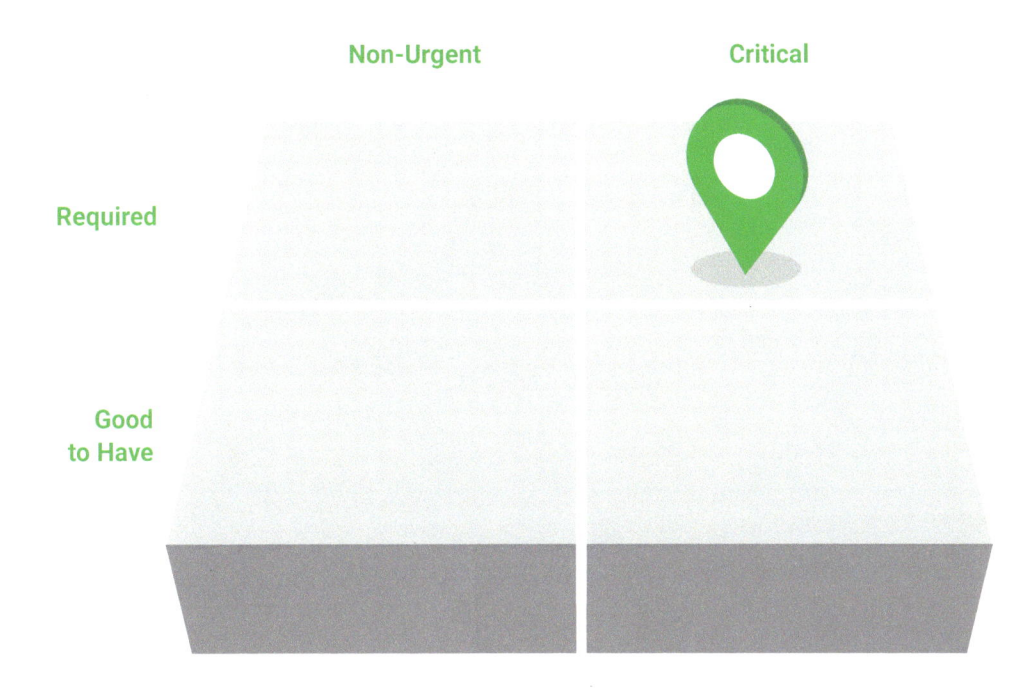

|  | Non-Urgent | Critical |
|---|---|---|
| **Required** |  | 📍 |
| **Good to Have** |  |  |

# Evaluate

Is your product a breakthrough or unique? A useful approach is to think of your breakthrough in the context of "the 3Ds": What unique combination of (D)iscontinuous innovation, (D)efensible technology, and (D)isruptive business model are you bringing to bear and what makes it truly compelling—not just to you and your colleagues, but to your most skeptical customer?

- **Discontinuous innovations** offer transformative benefits over the status quo by looking at a problem differently.

- **Defensible technology** offers intellectual property that can be protected to create a barrier to entry and an unfair competitive advantage.

- **Disruptive business models** yield value and cost rewards that help catalyze the growth of a business.

# Measure

Estimate the potential adoption ratio based on pains and gains. How do the gains offset the pains associated with adoption? Most entrepreneurs are so focused on the features they deliver they forget to examine how hard it will be for customers to learn to use their product.

- Gains can be measured in revenue, cost savings, time, people, competitive advantage, and reputation.
- Pains that obstruct adoption can include inertia, switching costs, startup risks, training costs, unclear economic benefits, or the relative cost of making no change or selecting alternative products.

## GAIN/PAIN RATIO

The **GAIN** delivered to the customer  VS  The **PAIN** and cost for the customer to adopt

# Build

Once you have gone through the defining, evaluating, and measuring steps, you are ready to build your value proposition using the following framework, filling in the blanks:

For _____(target customer)

Who are dissatisfied with _____ (current alternative)

Our product is a _____(new product)

That provides _____(key problem-solving capabilities)

Unlike _____(product(s) in the market).

# BENEFITS TO CONSIDER WHEN BUILDING YOUR VALUE PROPOSITION—BY STAKEHOLDER:

**Patients**
- Improved health
- Fewer refills/hospital visits
- Reduced procedures/expense

**Payers/Insurance/Medicare/Medicaid**
- More patient accountability
- Reduction in costs

**Strategic Acquirers***
- Large addressable market
- Quickly accretive
- Incremental revenues

**Clinicians**
- Improved outcomes
- Improved workflow/efficiency
- Fewer adverse events

**Funding sources**
- Well-protected intellectual property
- Low regulatory risk or short approval time
- Existing reimbursement code
- High investment return potential

---

* A strategic acquirer is a buyer operating in the same industry/business as the target company. This buyer typically will pay a premium for the business because it attributes value to existing products or services and/or adds a complementary business to its existing operations.

# CASE STUDY
## HypoCore/Novocore Medical

**The Problem**
- Low percentage of neurologically intact survivors after suffering outpatient cardiac arrest

**Clinical benefit**
- Therapeutic hypothermia has been proven to increase neurologically intact survival rates for out-of-the-hospital cardiac arrest patients.

**Unmet Need**
- Reduce time from cardiac arrest to initiating therapeutic hypothermia (TH) for first responders treating cardiac arrest. Several good product alternatives for in-hospital administration of therapeutic hypothermia are already on the market. First responders have started making attempts to initiate TH in the field but lack the tools to do it effectively and consistently.

**Specifications for the solution**
(based on stakeholder interviews)
- No external power source required
- Compact to fit in ambulance, helicopter, or paramedic kit
- Delivers consistently cold therapy to the patient
- Available on demand
- Little to no impact on existing EMS protocols/process
- Cost effective for EMS
- Will not require costly clinical trial for regulatory approval
- Single use disposable but robust for EMS use

**Solution**
- HypoCore: An innovative rapid chilling device that cools saline during the infusion process to induce therapeutic hypothermia.

**Value proposition** – (Compact statement)
- HypoCore is a portable first responder solution for inducing therapeutic hypothermia in the field by administering cooled saline for up to 30 minutes employing standard IV tubing and with no external power.

---

**Value Proposition** – (Extented version that might be used in some product promotional literature)

- HypoCore helps Emergency Medical Service first responders save lives. Our patented product is an innovative rapid chilling device that cools saline during the infusion process to induce therapeutic hypothermia. HypoCore is ready on demand, attaches in-line to standard IV tubing, and instantly cools saline for up to 30 minutes without any external power. It is easily stored in ambulances, fire trucks, and helicopters and can be carried anywhere EMS personnel go.

# SECTION 3

# BUSINESS CASE VALIDATION

Now that you have validated that the problem you are interested in solving has traction from users and payers, it is time to find out if your project will attract the necessary funds to reach the market.

Understanding the risk/reward profile of your project is important if you will need to raise funds, as will be the case for many medical technologies. Even in those circumstances where you will not need to raise either angel or venture funding (both are explained in the following section), you need to evaluate the potential market size for your product to determine what commercial structure will be required to bring it to market. This also applies if the product is going to be licensed to a company, as you need to know the market potential to be able to discuss the licensing terms.

✓ **Understand the size of the market you are entering**

✓ **Define the specific market you are targeting**

✓ **Appropriately price your product for this market**

## 3.1 MARKET SIZE

In order to understand the potential revenue of your company, you need to understand its market potential—the entire size of the market for a product. Market potential is usually measured either by sales value or sales volume.

Understanding market size also helps you distinguish between the addressable market, which is the total revenue opportunity for your product or service, and the available market, which is the portion of the addressable market for which you can realistically compete. Without a full understanding of market size, you may be conducting business in a market that is too small to make it commercially viable.

Often entrepreneurs talk about the size of the market for diabetes being $40 billion as if that represents an indication of the business opportunity. However, this figure does not indicate the market potential of the device, test, service, or drug that the opportunity represents but instead the entirely of all dollars spent on this disease each year.

We will start by introducing terminology related to market size that may figure in your conversations with investors.

**Total Available Market (TAM):** The total available market for a product or service. Also known as the **potential market**, this refers to the maximum potential sales if all patients/procedures/locations purchased a product.

Let's assume, as an example, that your company is developing a resorbable stent. The TAM is the market for all types of stents, approximately $9 billion. This market is further segmented into three categories: bare-metal, drug-eluting, and biodegradable.

**Serviceable Available Market (SAM):** This is the likely portion of the market to adopt your product and thus is smaller than the total available market. To define the SAM, you may have to consider the possible limitations that your product/company may have, such as pricing, geographical coverage, or approval/reimbursement restrictions.

Considering again our resorbable stent example, it is possible that reimbursement approval for your product will be limited to those patients who suffered restenosis or that the claims you made to receive regulatory approval narrow the market. It is also possible that your market introduction strategy limits the product to certain geographies.

**Target Market (TM):** Also known as the Serviceable Obtainable Market (SOM), this is the portion of the market that you expect to capture because your product is or will ultimately be (in a future generation) compelling for them.

There may be other competitors in the market with similar technology. To define the TM, it is important to understand the current competition as well as potential entrants into the market.

**Entry Market (EM):** This refers to the patient segment that most stands to benefit from your product (and is therefore most likely to drive clinician adoption).

The highly regulated medical field sometimes requires a special market entry strategy to reduce either the cost or the time to get a product approved. Your company may want to consider narrowing your target patient population to lower the costs of clinical trials, or impose a special designation that may shorten the length of the trial. This strategy could be very appealing to investors who otherwise will consider the endeavor too risky.

## Let's assume that you develop a product that eliminates CAUTIs (catheter-associated urinary tract infections).

**Some assumptions based on review of clinical literature:**

- CAUTI risk increases after 72 hours and increases dramatically after 7 days
- Assumes only one catheter per patient stay

**TAM - 60M patients**
All patients admitted into the hospital

**SAM - 40M patients**
Total number of Foley catheters sold to in-patient hospitals today

**TM - 2M patients**
The portion of critical care patients that stay in the ICU more than 72 hours

**EM - 250K patients**
Patients in neuro ICU, burn units, and trauma ICU - this is the most likely segment to adopt because they have the longest catheter indwelling period

*For illustrative/educational purposes only*

3.1 MARKET SIZE

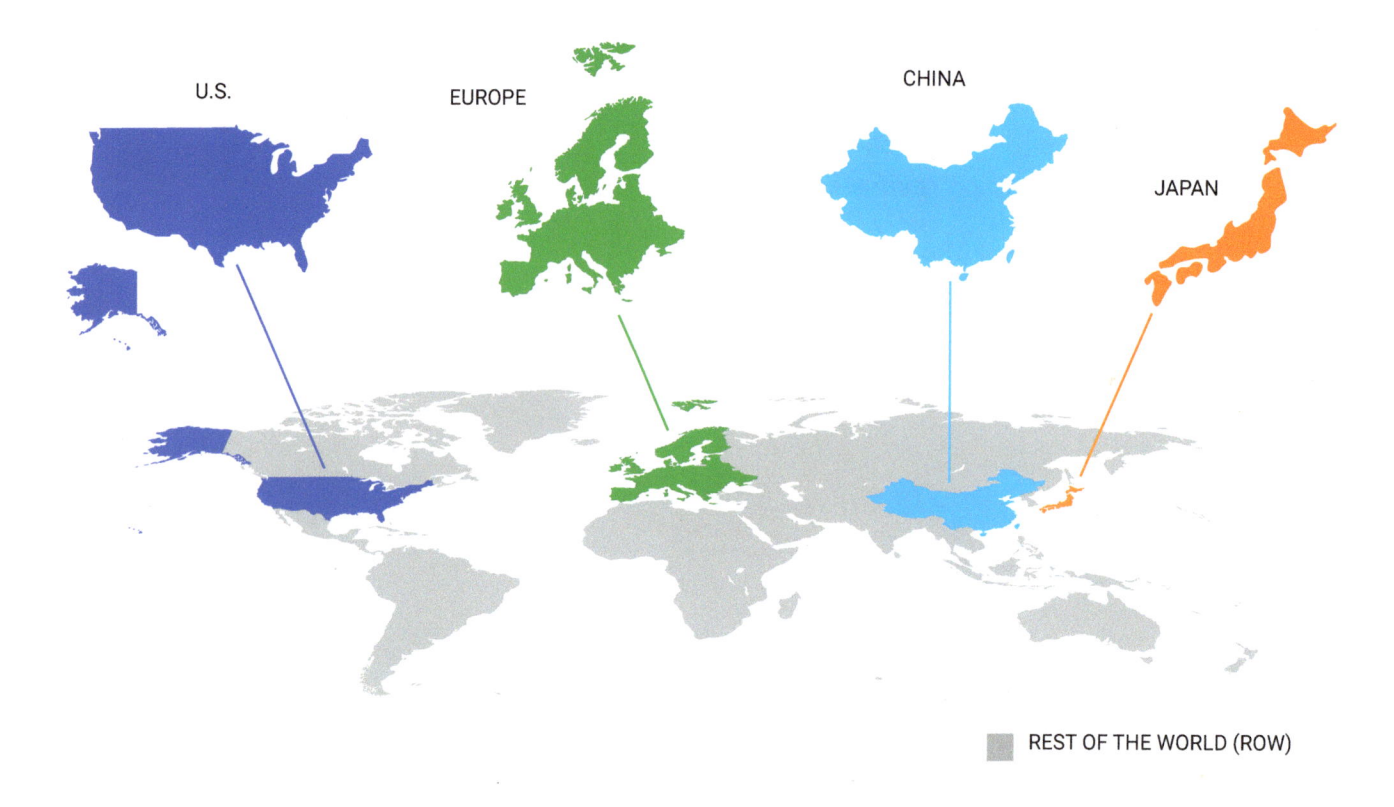

## What units describe your market?

Also important to your business case is determining the units you will use to describe your market. Dollars? Number of devices or tests? Or number of patients? For example, if your product is a new CT scanner that will reduce radiation by 75%, it is important to know how many units the opportunity represents. How many hospitals with scanners are in the **U.S.**? What about **EUROPE**, **CHINA**, **JAPAN** and what we call the **REST OF THE WORLD (ROW)**? What is the installed base of CT scanners?

If the product is a new diagnostic test, it would be important to know the patient population that will require the test, the frequency of the test, and whether it is just a screening or one that will require continual follow-up. For a drug, the patient population is key.

In the market segment example in the section above, you may have noticed that we referred to the markets for the catheter product in terms of patients—not dollars. This is a best practice when doing an early market evaluation.

Numbers are always more representative than dollars, but the number of units must also be accompanied by the unit selling price. Here a new acronym is useful: ASP, or average selling price. The ASP for a product does not represent the net price that the product will command in the market.

## 3.2 WHO WILL PAY?

Before we dive into the topic of pricing, it's important to understand who will actually be paying for your product or service. As you might expect, it's incredibly challenging to develop a viable business if nobody is willing to pay for your product or service.

Elective procedures like Botox, for example, may be paid for out of pocket by customers/patients. Patients might also pay out of pocket for medications, tests, equipment, or procedures if not covered by insurance or if the patient does not have insurance.

Often providers are reimbursed for services through one or more "payers":

- Federal and state government programs, such as Medicare and Medicaid
- Private insurance programs offered through employment and individual plans, such as Blue Cross Blue Shield

A smaller percentage of the bill, known as a co-payment, is often paid directly by the insured patient. Notably, this payment billed to the patient with commercial insurance is often separate from and in addition to a monthly charge to stay covered, commonly known as a premium.

Every new product needs to receive coverage by the appropriate payer. For hospital-based products such as medical devices, the hospital value purchase committee makes the decision based on health care economics. They asses whether the proposed product reduces costs, improves margins, or improves outcome or other quality metrics. For drugs, hospitals receive a lump sum for treating a specific condition. In the case of a new drug, payment coverage is often related to the drug's ability to demonstrate a substantial clinical improvement over existing treatment options.

Reimbursement often involves a payment as a percentage of the total cost and is usually impacted by standards set by Centers for Medicare and Medicaid Services (CMS). The reimbursement amount is also based on negotiations between an office practice and regional insurance companies with which they contract. Insurance companies typically follow CMS recommendations on reimbursement.

CMS payments are based on the Current Procedural Terminology (CPT®) codes issued by American Medical Association (AMA). You will hear this acronym, CPT, often. These codes are used by medical professionals to document and report medical, surgical, radiology, laboratory, anesthesiology, and evaluation and management services. CPT is divided into three categories of codes.

- **Category I:** Procedures that are consistent with contemporary medical practice and are widely performed.
- **Category II:** Supplementary tracking codes that can be used for performance measures.
- **Category III:** Temporary codes for emerging technology, services, and procedures.

Understanding provider reimbursement on some level will be important to the development of your business model.

## 3.3. OTHER MODELS

While it's true that your product ultimately needs to be paid for by someone, that may not directly relate to how you or your organization earns revenue. There are other successful models of which you should be aware, including:

**Private labeling:** In this arrangement, your company manufactures a product that is sold to another company and labeled with the name of the acquiring company. Products that are natural extensions of other product lines are ideal private-label products. Under this model, it's possible to get a large order or a commitment before your product has actually been produced. This could allow you to borrow money or possibly get extended terms you're your manufacturer. Operating costs are low with this model, as your business is structured around delivering all your products to one customer.

**Strategic acquisition:** Another company may want to acquire your company to round out its product offerings or as a complement to its primary product line. For example, if you have a software product that is complementary to the interpretation of CT images, the large CT manufacturers (known as strategics) might choose to acquire your company.

**Licensing:** Another way to get your medical device technology into the commercial market is to license your technology to another company. This is a very common strategy with drug and biologics development, which are incredibly expensive to develop all the way through human trials and product launch, and thus beyond the capabilities of most startups. Similarly, many medical devices are technically complex, requiring numerous patents covering the structure, function, and methods of using the device. Large device companies may choose to pursue licensing your technology, rather than buying product from you, in order to control the supply chain, quality system, and regulatory structure, as well as align design characteristics of the actual product to fit with their branding.

## 3.4. THE SHIFT TO VALUE-BASED HEALTH CARE

The U.S. health care system is experiencing a gradual transition from a **fee-for-service (FFS)** reimbursement model to **value-based care**, a reimbursement methodology that encourages health care providers to deliver the best quality care at the most reasonable cost. In this new model, instead of being paid by the number of visits and tests they order, providers are paid based on measures of clinical quality and cost.

This shift may influence your business model as well as your approach to product cost and reimbursement. While it is possible for a business to appear more viable in one environment than another, a product and its related business model would ideally be successful in both environments.

Value-based health care represents an enormous business opportunity for companies willing to develop value-based strategies and to build the capabilities necessary to execute those strategies successfully. Value-based strategies include:

**Value-Based Solutions:** Supplementing a traditional product offering with new products or services designed to improve health outcomes and/or lower costs. Value-improvement strategies focus on providing a comprehensive solution rather than a stand-alone product.

**Value measurement:** In the age of big data, strategies that leverage systematic value measurement are especially relevant to companies that are trying to introduce new devices or therapies.

**Value-based care delivery:** Certainly it is not feasible for most medical innovation companies to also deliver care, however it may be a viable strategy for companies focused on conditions like diabetes or cardiac care in which devices play a key role in the ongoing management of the disease.

## Addressing Health Care Economics

The relatively new discipline of Health Care Economics is concerned with optimizing efficiency, effectiveness, value, and behavior in the production and consumption of health and health care. This may have positive and negative effects on your business. Important to note:

- Hospitals have created Value Analysis Committees (VAC)—advisory groups that decide what medical devices make it onto the hospital's shelves. Composed of hospital administrators, care providers, and other stakeholders, VACs want to see a clear definition of value, e.g., safety, comparative effectiveness, process improvement, and quality. (Only when devices become commoditized can the decisions move to price.)

- The widespread adoption of predictive diagnostic tests by physicians only occurs when they are reimbursed by public or private health insurance. Therefore, for companies developing these tests, securing coverage by private and public payers can be the final, make-or-break hurdle before their tests can enter the marketplace.

- Reimbursement of high-cost drugs, including personalized medicine, poses a difficult problem in health care, especially with immuno-oncology drugs where the cost to hospitals may run close to $1 million per patient. Reimbursement could be delayed until the benefits are sufficiently demonstrated.

# 3.5 PRICING STRATEGY

Pricing a new product is one of the hardest decisions that any entrepreneur will face. You don't want to leave money on the table by pricing below the value your product provides to the stakeholders. However, you also don't want to price yourself out of the market. For medical innovators in particular, pricing a new solution can be even more challenging, due to a number of factors not present in other markets such as the role and influence of numerous stakeholders involved in access and utilization decisions. Another key factor leading to complexity of pricing decisions is reimbursement and funding.

We will approach pricing strategy from these three verticals:

- Value based pricing
- Competitive pricing (commodities)
- Reimbursement-driven pricing

No matter which pricing strategy you employ, start by calculating the price for which your company will achieve equilibrium (no profit or loss) or a desired level of profitability (e.g., 10% operating income before taxes) for the number of units you estimated for your target market. You will need to understand the direct and indirect costs of developing and selling your product, such as manufacturing, employees, marketing, distribution, and operating costs.

## Value-based pricing

Value-based pricing (VBP) is a pricing strategy that sets prices primarily, but not exclusively, on the perceived or estimated value to the payer rather than on the cost of the product or on the prices of competing products. Entrepreneurs often think that they will obtain higher market share (the percentage of total sales volume in a market captured by a brand) by lowering prices. In many cases the opposite occurs, and a price war ensues.

Value-based pricing requires a health economics study to demonstrate why your product will have an overall lower cost for the health care system despite a high product price. Pricing a laboratory test at $700, for example, when most tests are below $30 requires demonstrating other areas of savings for the hospital or payer.

## Competitive pricing

For a commodity (an interchangeable good as distinguished from a service or a consumable), a low-price strategy may allow you to beat out your competitors and achieve an important market share. Price is typically an important component in the buyer decision process for undifferentiated products such as syringes, many routine laboratory tests, some orthopedic devices, urinary catheters, etc.

Bundled sales is another mechanism for staying competitive on price. This may included offering a range of products as a package, where the pricing of the individual components of the offer is obscure or unspecified. Bundling also simplifies administration for hospitals and payers. This approach is particularly advantageous for large medical device suppliers like GE, Abbot, Medtronic, and others.

**A WINNING MODEL: THE RAZOR-RAZORBLADE**

Certain products may enable what is known as a "razor-razorblade" model, which involves selling an item at a low price, sometimes even at a loss, in order to sell complementary or consumable products later. The name refers to the original use by the Gillette Company to sell hand-held razors at cost and then make a high margin of profit by selling the blades.

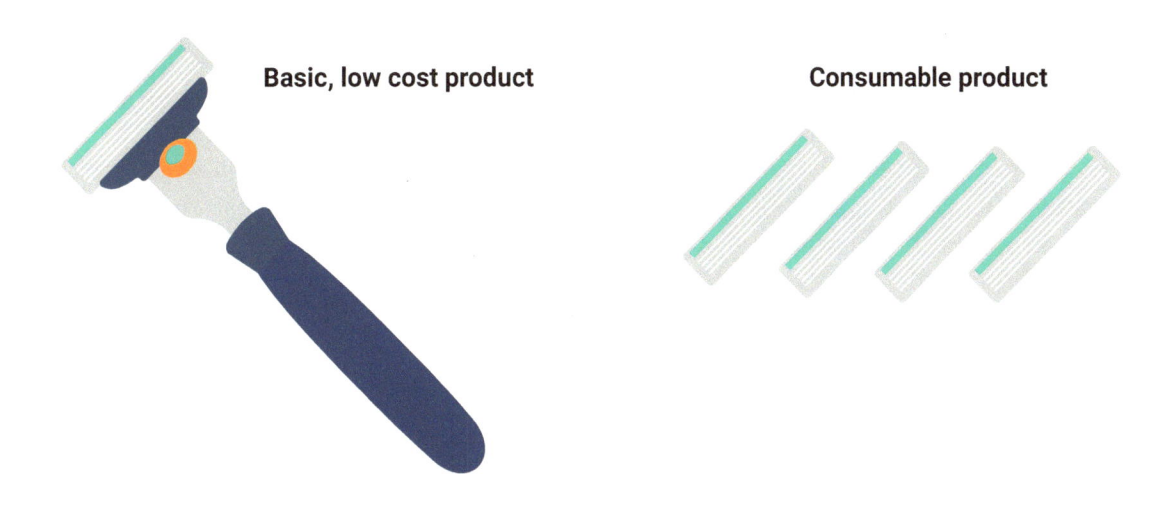

**Basic, low cost product**　　　　　**Consumable product**

## Reimbursement-driven pricing

As noted above, value-based care has emerged as an alternative to and eventual replacement for fee-for-service models. By 2025, value-based care delivery will account for 70 percent of total healthcare spend, and various forms of capitation and bundled payments will be ubiquitous.[7] Bundled payment arrangements are designed to pay multiple providers for coordinating the total amount of services required for a single, pre-defined episode of care.

In addition to competing with other products, your company is also competing with facilities and physicians for reimbursement sharing. As you develop your product and your business model, you must decide where you want to compete, how you want to compete, with what offerings, and with which partners.

[7] https://www.oliverwyman.com/our-expertise/insights/2014/oct/value-based-care-a-guide-for-medical-device-companies.html

## 3.6 YOUR FINANCIAL MODEL

If a capital raise is in your future, then you will need to share a financial model with investors as part of your pitch. A financial model projects the performance of your company for years to come and includes core financial statements, such as your business's income statement, balance sheet, statement of retained earnings, and the cash flow statement for your historical financials. (See the appendix for an example of these financial documents and how they fit together.)

Of course, at the time of your pitch, your business might not have historical financials to which you can refer, especially if you have just entered or are entering the market. Nonetheless, you will need to be able to make sound predictions of your company's potential income and expenses. These numbers should be presented as an Income Statement, also known as a Profit and Loss statement, or "P&L."

If your income statement is based solely on projections, you may refer to it as a *pro forma*, which literally means "as a matter of form." In the world of investing, *pro forma* refers to a method of calculation that places emphasis on present or projected figures.

**ACME MEDICAL**
**STATEMENT OF INCOME**
Year Ending December 31, 2019

| | |
|---|---:|
| **Revenues** | $ 1,000,000 |
| **Cost of goods sold** | 200,000 |
| Gross profit | 800,000 |
| **Operating expenses** | |
| Selling, general, and administrative expense | 357,700 |
| Interest expense | 20,000 |
| Depreciation and amortization expense | 5,200 |
| Operating income | 437,100 |
| Interest income | 20,000 |
| **Net earnings before taxes** | 437,100 |
| Income tax expense | 240,000 |
| **Net income** | $ 197,000 |

## SECTION 4

# UNDERSTANDING INVESTMENT AND FINANCING

Early stage companies need funding in order to commercialize their ideas. These funds can come in the form of both non-dilutive and dilutive sources, as well as from a spectrum of entities. Funding tends to progress from smaller investment amounts during the earlier, riskier stages to larger investments from more substantial investors in the later, less risky stages (we will cover ways to reduce risk in Part II of this guide). Funding events are usually characterized as "rounds" and may be divided into different phases also known as "tranches" (Tranche is a French word meaning "slice" or "portion").

# 4.1 NON-DILUTIVE FINANCING

**Dilution** is a reduction in the ownership percentage of a share of stock caused by the issuance of new shares. Therefore, **non-dilutive** funding refers to financing that does not require the sale of your company's shares. The use of non-dilutive funds as a component of your financing strategy has many benefits. Non-dilutive funds allow founding teams and existing shareholders to retain company ownership and control. They may also provide:

- Critical cash to support your company's development

- Important validation of the team and technology

- Access to clinical expertise and stakeholders, increasing your chances of translational success

- A bridge between early-stage research and venture capital-ready technologies

## Types of non-dilutive funding

**Government research grants:** The National Institute of Health (NIH) is a good example, where companies can compete for R01 and R21 grants alongside traditional University applicants. These government research grants typically fund basic research or its commercial translation.

**Government industry grants:** These grants typically emphasize the commercialization of research; the application often requires a strong market argument for the future product. The Small Business Innovation Research (SBIR) program is a good example of a highly competitive program that typically funds commercialization activities.

**Foundations:** Foundations are becoming an increasingly important driver of medical biotechnology innovation, in particular innovations focused on improving the health of individuals afflicted with a specific disease. Foundations also provide a conduit to clinical expertise and potential access to patients and stakeholders.

**Industry partnerships:** Typical industry partnerships involve a transfer of technology from a small biotech, for example, to a large company in return for cash and/or co-development rights. These partnerships can provide significant cash flows and often represent the first major validation of the technology. Note that such transactions usually involve a license or option-to-license intellectual property.

**Venture Debt:** Venture debt or venture lending is a type of debt financing provided to venture-backed companies by specialized banks or non-bank lenders to fund working capital or capital expenses, such as purchasing equipment. Unlike traditional bank lending, venture debt is available to startups and growth companies that do not have positive cash flows or significant assets to use as collateral.

**Revenue:** Building a company with an immediate revenue stream is not always feasible. But for some companies, such as biotech firms will little to no regulatory involvement, establishing customers to test and use early prototypes is possible. For firms with significantly more regulatory barriers, revenue can sometimes be generated through auxiliary products or services, such as contract research or consulting. In the latter case, founding teams must be careful that this does not become such a significant distraction as to create significant delays for the primary product/company goals.

| PRE-SEED | SEED/ANGELS | VENTURE CAPITAL (SERIES A, B, etc.) | IPO/ACQUISITION |
|---|---|---|---|
| • Angel investment (< $500k)<br>• Self-investment, friends and family<br>• SBIR grants, NIH research grants, and other non-dilutive funding | • Angel Groups (~$500k-$1M)<br>• Investor networks<br>• Banks | • Venture Capital ($1M - $10M) | • Private Equity<br>• Merger/Acquisitions<br>• Strategic Acquirers<br>• Sovereign Wealth Fund<br>• Initial Public Offering (IPO) |

## 4.2 DILUTIVE FINANCING

**Angels** and **venture capital (VC)** firms are the predominant forms of dilutive financing in the U.S.

**Angel investors** are usually an association or group of individuals looking to diversify their portfolios and who have affinity for a specific sector. Angels have become one of the few available vehicles to fund early startup companies where the risk profile is high due to the early stage of the company. The terms are less onerous than those offered by VC firms and the funding is relatively modest, up to a couple of million, although lately we have seen funding of seven-figure deals. Angels usually invest seed capital or Series A funding. Their goal is to de-risk the project enough to have VCs take over. (A "Series A" round is the name typically given to a company's first significant round financing. The name refers to the class of preferred stock sold to investors in exchange for their investment.)

**Venture capital** is financing that investors provide to startup companies; venture capital firms, in general, raise hundreds of millions of dollars from family offices, wealthy individuals, and pension funds. Due to the size of their funds, they tend to invest in Series A or later. As a rule of thumb, a VC firm has several funds investing in 15-20 companies each. Valuations depend on the potential market and number of years to reach the market, but they expect a 10X return for A rounds. They invest in Series A and higher with the goal of selling the company to an established medical company or getting the company to an initial public offering (IPO) on the stock market.

VC firms and angel groups usually join forces with other firms to share the risk. In general, they are very regionally oriented and seldom invest outside of their region, unless they like the prospect a lot and the early stage company is willing to relocate.

Large medical industry firms also have their venture arms, which in general co-invest with VC firms. As of late, some pharma companies have decided to bypass VC firms and make strategic investments themselves in early stage companies. We haven't seen the same trend for medical devices, however.

**SECTION 5**

# BRINGING IT ALL TOGETHER— YOUR BUSINESS MODEL

In its simplest terms, a business model is the underlying economic logic that explains how a company can deliver value to customers at an appropriate cost. It is, in essence, a description of how your business runs.

Now that you understand the key elements to consider as you develop your product and your company, it's time to take a holistic view—to see what you may have missed, ensure that every element is addressed (not just those of most interest or with existing expertise), or even to compare your model to others.

R&D

MANUFACTURING

INTELLECTUAL PROPERTY

DISTRIBUTION

USERS

PATIENTS

UNIQUE VALUE PROPOSITION

PAYMENT & REIMBURSEMENT

MARKET

REGULATORY

INVESTMENT

SECTION 5: BRINGING IT ALL TOGETHER—YOUR BUSINESS MODEL

## SECTION 6

# COMMERCIALIZATION: AN EXERCISE IN DE-RISKING

In Part II we will focus our effort on understanding what it takes to bring a medical product to market. Commercialization is a long and perilous road; entrepreneurs must have a clear understanding of the risks involved and develop mitigation strategies.

The most common risks involve regulations, reimbursement, intellectual property (IP), technology validation, market risk, scaling-up manufacturing, management team challenges, and funding. Each one of these topics would be a book in itself; we will provide a short introduction of each risk.

## 6.1 FDA MEDICAL DEVICE REGULATORY CLASSIFICATIONS

In the U.S., if your product meets the definition of a medical device[1], there are Food and Drug Administration (FDA) requirements that apply. The rules that apply to your medical device depend on how your product is classified.

The FDA generally classifies medical devices based on the risks associated with the device and by evaluating the level of regulation that provides a reasonable assurance of the device's safety and effectiveness.

Devices are classified into one of three regulatory classes: Class I, Class II, or Class III. Class I includes devices with the lowest risk to the patient and Class III includes those with the greatest risk. Device classification depends on both the intended use of the device and also upon specific indications for use.

A basic understanding of regulatory product classification will be invaluable to your efforts to bring your product to market. Classification matters because it will:

1. Determine what you have to do before you can sell your product (i.e., the type of premarketing submission/application required for FDA clearance to market)

2. Help you establish what is required during product development and design controls.

3. Play a role in the investment required to bring your product to market

4. Help you determine how long it will take to have a product ready for the market

### REGULATION OUTSIDE THE U.S.

If you are intending to market your product globally, you should be aware of the various sanitary registration processes and how they differ.

In the E.U., for example, CE mark (an acronym for "conformité européenne") approval is the mandatory requirement of medical products and certifies that a product has met E.U. health, safety, and environmental requirements. A CE mark only requires proof of safety and that the device performs in a manner consistent with the manufacturer's intended use, thus the timeline for obtaining a CE mark has been typically much shorter than the timeline for gaining FDA regulatory approval.

Outside the E.U., the regulatory approval process is on a country-by-country basis—you will need to comply with whatever requirements are mandated for your device for each country in which you intend to market the device. Know that approval processes for drugs, however, are generally much more harmonized globally than medical devices; many of the processes to approve drugs in the E.U. are similar to those of the FDA, for example.

---

[1] https://www.fda.gov/MedicalDevices/DeviceRegulationandGuidance/Overview/ClassifyYourDevice/default.htm

## Examples of Medical Device Classifications

| Regulatory Classification | Devices |
|---|---|
| **Class I:** Considered to be at the lowest level of risk of all medical devices and are therefore required to comply with the lowest level of regulatory control | • Tongue depressors<br>• Gowns<br>• Dental floss |
| **Class II:** Considered to be at slightly higher risk than Class I devices and therefore require more stringent regulatory controls to provide assurance of their effectiveness and safety | • Cardiovascular guidewire<br>• CT scanner<br>• Medical laser |
| **Class III:** Considered to be at the highest risk and therefore require more stringent regulatory controls to provide assurance of their effectiveness and safety | • Stents<br>• Pacemakers<br>• Cancer diagnostics |

The class to which your device is assigned determines, among other things, the type of review process you will need to undergo to receive FDA clearance to market. There are two major review processes:

- **Premarket Notification,** which is commonly referred to as the "510(k) process." Clearance of a Premarket Notification submission confers permission to market the new device. By legal definition, it is not an "approval" process (under U.S. law, devices considered Class I products can be sold without approval from the FDA), but rather is classified as "cleared". A 510(k) typically requires no clinical trials. Instead, you will demonstrate that your medical device is similar to a previously approved product.[2]

- **Premarket Approval,** known by its submission acronym "PMA." The PMA process is based on a demonstration of safety and effectiveness through adequate and well-controlled clinical trials. A successful PMA submission results in approval of the new device. Most Class III devices must undergo a stringent PMA process, which requires clinical and laboratory studies, and extensive data, including information on manufacturing processes. Know that a PMA process can be very lengthy and therefore costly; it can take years to complete the necessary trials, submit your PMA, and receive approval.

Depending on the claims you make about your device or diagnostic product, it could be classified as Class II or III. For example, a software application that aids radiologists in detecting lung cancer would be considered Class II and require a 510(k), whereas a software application that claims independent detection of lung cancer will require a PMA. Similarly, a diagnostic test for cancer or a myocardial infarction will require a PMA.

---

[2] Some devices requiring Premarket Notification are subject to conformance with "Special Controls." Special Controls can be almost anything deemed necessary by FDA's Center for Devices and Radiologic Health (CDRH), which is responsible for the regulation of medical devices, and may include specialized labeling, conformance to specific standards, etc.

Entirely new devices (those with no predicates) are automatically considered Class III. To ease the approval process for lower-risk devices, however, the FDA created a new classification called De Novo Class I or II. The manufacturer must submit a De Novo request for the FDA to make a classification determination as either Class I or II. If the FDA rejects the classification, the product automatically requires a PMA.

How does the FDA clearance/approval process affect the likelihood of your product to succeed—or for your company to receive funding? The FDA risk relates to the time and cost required to bring the project to market. Class II 510(k) products, for example, are subject to a 90-day review period, while Class III products have a one-year review timeline once the PMA is submitted. Investors are only willing to pay for high-risk projects if the market opportunity is large enough to justify the risk.

## IS YOUR PRODUCT EXEMPT?

Medical innovations are sometimes considered exempt from both processes, particularly Class I devices and occasionally those classified as Class II. Exempt devices are sufficiently well known, and their safety and effectiveness are established, thus requiring no premarket review by the Agency. They are still subject to general regulations such as proper labeling, manufacturing best practices, and investigation of adverse events.

Visit the FDA website[3] for a full listing of 510(k) exempt devices. Keep in mind, if you are adding new technology to an exempt device (e.g., electronics or robotics), you will likely be subject to a review process.

[3] http://www.accessdata.fda.gov/scripts/cdrh/cfdocs/cfpcd/315.cfm

## 6.2 REIMBURSEMENT

Health care providers are paid by private insurance companies or government payers through a system of reimbursement. They provide medical services to a patient and then file for reimbursement for those services with the insurance company or government agency.

### Health care spending distribution in the U.S.[4]

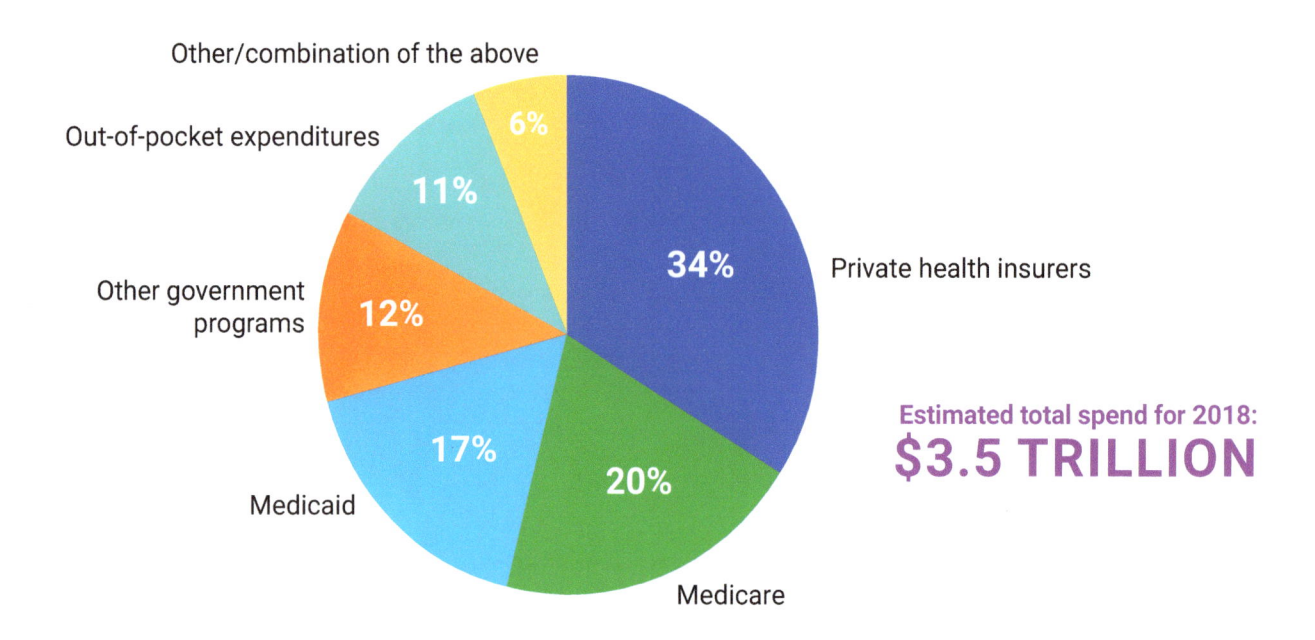

- Private health insurers: 34%
- Medicare: 20%
- Medicaid: 17%
- Other government programs: 12%
- Out-of-pocket expenditures: 11%
- Other/combination of the above: 6%

**Estimated total spend for 2018:**
**$3.5 TRILLION**

It is well known that the cost of health care is increasing faster than the Gross Domestic Product (GDP) and reaching levels that will be impossible to maintain as the population ages. At the same time, technology is making it possible to extend the productive lives of patients. Lifestyle issues are creating additional burdens on the medical system with the increase of chronic conditions such as diabetes, cardiovascular disease, and cancer. Health care systems are feeling more financial pressure than ever before.

As a result, the U.S. health care system is gradually shifting from traditional fee-for-service reimbursement models to reimbursement programs that reward health care providers for the quality of care that they give to patients. Value-based care aims to advance the triple aim of providing better care for individuals, improving population health management strategies, and reducing health care costs.

[4] https://www.statista.com/statistics/237043/us-health-care-spending-distribution

Value-based reimbursements are calculated by using numerous measures of quality and determining the overall health of populations. Value-based care is driven by data because providers must report to payers on specific metrics and demonstrate improvement. Thus, under the new models, providers are incentivized to use evidence-based medicine, engage patients, upgrade health IT, and use data analytics in order to get paid for their services. Providers are rewarded for delivering more coordinated, appropriate, and effective care to patients.

As patients are being treated differently and providers are being reimbursed differently, a whole new set of risks and opportunities will emerge for prescription benefit managers (PBMs), drug distributors, life science data players, and medical device innovators. The key to winning in the value-based health care market will be replacing the transactional, unit-cost model with integrated solutions that improve cost and quality. What can your company offer to improve outcomes, patient experiences, and/or cost of treating diseases? Can your product help providers deliver care more effectively and efficiently?

## 6.3 INTELLECTUAL PROPERTY (IP)

Protecting your intellectual property gives you exclusive rights to prevent others from making, using, or selling your patented invention. IP is essential to protecting your competitive advantage. Most investors will only put their money where IP exists, so protecting your intangible assets is worth your attention from the start.[5]

However, choosing which type of IP protection is right for your medical device is not always easy, especially when a device is eligible for more than one type of protection.

There are four major areas of IP law:

1. **Patents:** A patent is a right granted to an inventor by the federal government that permits the inventor to exclude others from making, selling, or using the invention for a period of time. There are two types of patents: **utility patents** protect the way an invention works, and **design patents** protect the appearance of an object. Determination of patentability can be very complex and should be reviewed by an IP expert. Learn more at this link.[6]

2. **Copyright:** Copyright's purpose is to protect works of authorship from being copied. It is customary to copyright the software used in medical devices or in managing medical processes. Also, the artwork and text on your product packaging, instructions leaflets, advertising, and website copy is likely to be protected by copyright.

---

[5] Note that there are both domestic and international processes to protect IP, and they are not the same. We are only speaking to IP as it relates to the U.S. in this guide, but you should be aware of other protocols globally, depending on your intended market.

[6] https://youtu.be/qFRaamWjYGo

3. **Trademarks:** Trademarks can apply to medical devices in several ways. First, the name of the device, as well as any symbol or slogan used on or in connection with the product, that identifies the source of the product, may be protectable. Second, the aesthetic design of the device may be protectable as a particular type of trademark called "trade dress." In the U.S., trademark rights arise out of mere use of the trademark in commerce. Additional benefits accrue through registration of a trademark with the United States Patent and Trademark Office.[8]

4. **Trade secrets:** A trade secret is any confidential business information that provides a business competitive advantage or economic benefit by virtue of it not being publicly known. Trade secret protection arises under state common law and state statutes. While it's not feasible to lock all your secrets away in a vault, there are many ways you can protect your information, from labeling key documents as "confidential," "proprietary," "secret," etc., to ensuring access to electronic files are restricted by standard security procedures such as password protection. A trade secret does not have a definite term like a patent, but rather lasts indefinitely unless and until the protected information is made available to the public.

## FREEDOM TO OPERATE

A patent issue gives you the right to prevent others from copying your invention, but it does not give you the right to practice your patent, as it can possibly infringe upon previously-issued patents. Determining freedom to operate is usually quite expensive and not in the realm of early-stage companies. However, some projects where the freedom to operate is not certain may discourage investment, especially those that require a large investment to bring to market.

**A WORD OF CAUTION**

As you pursue conversations with stakeholders, possible investors, or personnel from other companies, be mindful of what you are disclosing. Be sure to issue confidentiality agreements to anyone with whom you discuss your technology. Share incrementally as the relationship progresses and only if truly necessary.

---

[8] https://www.mddionline.com/which-type-ip-protection-right-your-medical-device

## 6.4 TECHNOLOGY VALIDATION

Validating your technology will require a variety of tests; the tests you choose and how they are executed are critical to the success of your product and business. Many early-stage projects fail to advance because the experiment conducted was not what we refer to as "The Killer Experiment."

The Killer Experiment is an experiment or set of experiments intentionally aimed at pressure testing critical features, attributes, or requirements of your envisioned product in as little time and with as few resources as possible. In short, this experiment can serve to "kill" a project that is unlikely to succeed before significant resources are put into developing and perfecting the technology. The goal: leave as little doubt as possible that technology is going to work *and work better* than currently available solutions or treatments. A killer experiment should have very tight controls to ensure that interpretation of the data is definitive.

The Killer Experiment is an important next step in your go-to-market timeline and should not be designed in a vacuum. Talk with potential investors and/or strategic acquirers. What will they want to see in an experiment to justify them putting their capital at risk? It is also important to ask your stakeholders what it would take to use your product. Depending on the stage of your technology, the burden of proof required to demonstrate feasibility, your regulatory strategy, etc., the Killer Experiment may be a pre-clinical or clinical study, freedom to operate, scale-up manufacturing, market acceptance, or the elimination of a risk with which an investor may be concerned.

For Class III devices (PMA) and drugs, for example, the main goal of pre-clinical studies is to determine safety in human use (known as first-in-man studies). These studies are seen as a value inflexion point by investors and strategics. For diagnostic test technology, the degree of validation required depends on the product claims. If the product claims to be a diagnostic aid, where the final responsibility resides in the doctor, the burden of proof is substantially is less than that of products indicated to provide a diagnosis, as the latest poses a higher risk for the patient.

### REPRODUCIBILITY OF RESULTS

One issue that often arises in discussions with investors at this early stage is **reproducibility of results.** Can the same results be obtained by a different group not involved in the project? Ideally, your experiments and the results you have obtained should be reproducible by a different group in a different organization. The ultimate seal of approval is often when a contract research organization (CRO) can duplicate the results; however, this is expensive and may be cost prohibitive for many early-stage companies.

As a project progresses in the development process, and as the technical risks decrease, investor appetite and valuation will increase. It is important that the project leaders have discussed with investors what tests and results they would like to see before they would consider the risk low enough to invest. A failure to do this may result in time and money spent on experiments that, although valuable, won't address the needs of investors.

## 6.5 MARKET RISK

As discussed, barriers to medical innovation include regulatory approval, reimbursement, clinical trials, and a complex sales channel strategy. We have also noted the major shifts in market dynamics as the health care industry transitions from a fee-for-service payment model to a value-based provider model.

Unfortunately, the risks don't end there. It's important to understand that the medical market itself is volatile and opportunities for funding can reflect these unpredictable shifts. In recent years we have seen new, innovative products lose their attractiveness due to disappointing clinical or commercial results elsewhere in a related area of the market. Technologies such as optical coherence tomography (OCT), monoclonal antibodies-based drugs, and diseases such Alzheimer's, obesity, and diabetes, for example, have suffered the ups and downs of the market. When you're ready to look for financing for your technology, know that fluctuations in the medical market may have an impact on the valuation of your company. (We will talk more about valuation shortly.)

Bringing complex medical technologies to market is typically not a straight-line exercise. In the last 10 years, very few medical companies, especially device and diagnostic companies, have been able to go directly to the stock market as an IPO (initial public offering), for example. Instead, investors are focused on maturing companies to the point that they are attractive to strategic acquirers ("strategics")— established companies willing to pay a premium for products that fit into their strategic plan. Strategics already have a foothold—and a sales channel—in the target market. To that end, it's important to identify and build relationships with potential acquirers from the beginning.

In the pharmaceutical industry, we have seen an interesting development in recent years: pharma companies are willing to compete with venture funds for drug assets, investing in promising, early-stage compounds and acting like a venture fund. We have not seen this approach in medical devices, however. Diagnostics, where investments to reach the market are lower and, in general, tied to a specific platform, are more likely to get licensed at an early stage.

In this challenging market environment, it best to be aware and arm your company with:

- A strong value proposition that's backed by data
- A knowledge of (and ideally relationships with) potential strategic acquirers
- A strong leadership team with an experienced CEO who knows how to navigate the market
- A scientific board that has extensive scientific and practical experience in the field

## 6.6 SCALE-UP MANUFACTURING

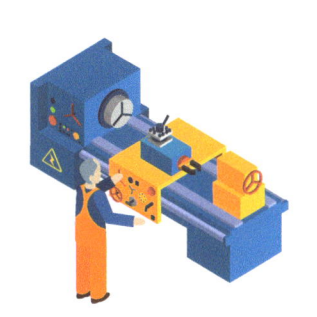

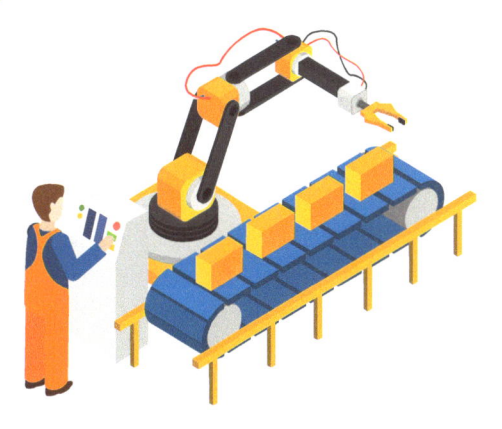

Most early-stage projects start from an invention or discovery at a university. Among the many questions that must answered in on the journey to commercialization is whether the product can be manufactured to a scale that meets profitable demand.

A concern for medical devices is whether they can be reduced in size to make a viable product. With pharmaceutical products, the processes for producing large quantities of a compound are different than those in the university lab—will different equipment, for example, mean different results?

Many medical products will scale up with success. However, investors will want to see evidence that a larger pilot batch can produce expected results. For those products where a new manufacturing process must be created and thus require a large initial investment, the promise of the gain (market opportunity) must be worth the pain (investment).

Finding contract manufacturers that are capable of producing your product in the appropriate quantities under the proper regulations will help to assure investors of the manufacturability, yields, predictability, quality, and cost of your product.

## 6.7 MANAGEMENT TEAM

Many early-stage companies fail to appreciate the value of a strong team that can raise funds and move the product forward. Finding the right-fit CEO who has a track record of raising funds is one of the most valuable investments that an early-stage company can make.

Bringing a medical product to market can be an exciting but harrowing journey. It requires a team that can adapt to the circumstances and pivot when necessary.

For example, we have seen projects proceed successfully through clinical trials and meet the stated goals of investors, only to lose the interest of strategic acquirers who have been spooked by unrelated events in the market. Sometimes companies face challenges with first-in-man studies, meeting FDA requirements, or receiving the right level of reimbursement from payers. In cases like these, the team must find a solution that can be financed with the resources available.

This is where an experienced CEO can make all the difference. In general, VCs like to invest in the product but also in the jockey. We have seen projects with excellent results stay in the university without funding until the proper CEO joins the team. And, because the initial role of the CEO for early-stage companies is to raise funds, it's important that the CEO is known by investors as someone with a proven track record. View this short video[1] to learn more about the CEO's role in a startup.

A chief technology officer (CTO) is also vital member of the leadership team. Because university professors and researchers rarely leave their post to join the startup, it is important to have a CTO who is familiar with the technology, such as a PhD student or postdoctoral researcher who worked on the project.

Early-stage companies should also strongly consider forming an advisory board of well-respected individuals in the field in order to gain credibility and stewardship, including technical and commercial advice and contacts.

[1] https://binged.it/2B4rxwf

# 6.8 VALUATION AND FUNDING

One of the major sources of friction between investors and early-stage companies is related to valuation. Valuation is the process of determining the value of an asset or company. More generally, it is As a judgment that someone makes about how much money something is worth.

There are generally two different perspectives on valuation.

- **Company view:** Early-stage companies see what they have accomplished, the number of years it took from initial research to this point, and how much money they have invested or received in governmental grants. Also, they consider the value of their technology as if it was already on the market.

- **Investor view:** VCs, on the other hand, see the technical and commercial risk ahead and the amount of money required to bring this product to the point that they will have a profitable exit for their investors. VCs in general look for 10X (ten times) return on their investment when they invest in series A (a company's first significant round of venture capital financing). They must consider the time to exit (sell their ownership of the company) and how much money they will have to invest through that exit.

> ### WHY VCS SEEK 10X RETURNS
> Investment firms typically have a spectrum of different investments in their portfolio. They know that for any fund to provide a decent return to their investors, they need to have one or two projects that will yield 10-fold returns to help supplant and offset some of their other projects that may yield only 3-fold returns as well as those that break even or worse. Another way to look at it: out of 10 companies in which a VC invests, only two will be profitable enough to make the entire investment effort worthwhile.

Multiple considerations play into what level of risk the investor is willing to shoulder. How early the company's product is in the development continuum, the commercial experience of the management team, and how much money is required to bring it to market, together with the possible exit price, are all factors that control the valuation.

Before we take a look at a hypothetical example, it's important understand some valuation terminology:

- **Pre-money valuation** refers to the valuation of the company prior to a financing transaction. With limited exceptions, the pre-money valuation + the amount invested in a financing deal = the post-money valuation.

- **Post-money valuation** is a company's value after outside financing and/or capital investments are added to its balance sheet.

- **Dilution** is a result of a reduction in the ownership percentage of a company, or shares of stock, due to the issuance of new equity shares by the company. When the number of shares increases, each stockholder owns a smaller, or diluted, percentage of the company. That being said, as the company continues to grow in value, smaller percentages will represent greater worth.

## An Exercise in Valuation

The following table demonstrates typical changes in value and ownership over the course of a company's funding cycle. For the sake of example, this is a simplified version of what is known as a **capitalization table** (or "cap table"), which provides an analysis of a company's percentages of ownership, equity dilution, and value of equity in each round of investment by founders, investors, and other owners.

Let's build a cap table for a hypothetical company, tranche by tranche, to see how dilution and company growth are part of the same continuum.

**Seed round**  The company raises $1M of seed funding in the first year at a 20% pre-money valuation.

| Seed funding: Year 1 | | |
|---|---|---|
| | | Valuation |
| Founders | 80% | $4M |
| Seed investors | 20% | $1M |
| Total | 100% | $5M |

6.8: VALUATION AND FUNDING | 42

**Series A** — In year three, the company receives $10M at a pre-money valuation of $10M, or $20M post-money valuation. This represents a dilution of $10/$20 = 50%.

|  | Seed funding: Year 1 | Valuation | Series A: Year 3 | Valuation |
|---|---|---|---|---|
| Founders | 80% | $4M | 40% | $8M |
| Seed investors | 20% | $1M | 10% | $2M |
| Series A Investors |  |  | 50% | $10M |
| Total | 100% | $5M | 100% | $20M |

**Series B** — The company raises a new round in year five of $20M at a pre-money valuation of $60M, or $80M post-money valuation, with a dilution of $20/$80=25%.

|  | Seed funding: Year 1 | Valuation | Series A: Year 3 | Valuation | Series B: Year 5 | Valuation |
|---|---|---|---|---|---|---|
| Founders | 80% | $4M | 40% | $8M | 30% | $24M |
| Seed investors | 20% | $1M | 10% | $2M | 7.5% | $6M |
| Series A Investors |  |  | 50% | $10M | 37.5% | $30M |
| Series B Investors |  |  |  |  | 25% | $20M |
| Total | 100% | $5M | 100% | $20M | 100% | $80M |

**Series C** — In year seven, the company raises a new round of funding of $25M at a pre-money valuation of $95M, or $120M post-money valuation, with a dilution of $25/$120 = 20.8%.

|  | Seed funding: Year 1 | Valuation | Series A: Year 3 | Valuation | Series B: Year 5 | Valuation | Series C: Year 7 | Valuation |
|---|---|---|---|---|---|---|---|---|
| Founders | 80% | $4M | 40% | $8M | 30% | $24M | 23.75% | $28.5M |
| Seed investors | 20% | $1M | 10% | $2M | 7.5% | $6M | 5.94% | $7.13M |
| Series A Investors |  |  | 50% | $10M | 37.5% | $30M | 29.69% | $35.63M |
| Series B Investors |  |  |  |  | 25% | $20M | 19.79% | $23.75M |
| Series C Investors |  |  |  |  |  |  | 20.83% | $25M |
| Total | 100% | $5M | 100% | $20M | 100% | $80M | 100% | $120M |

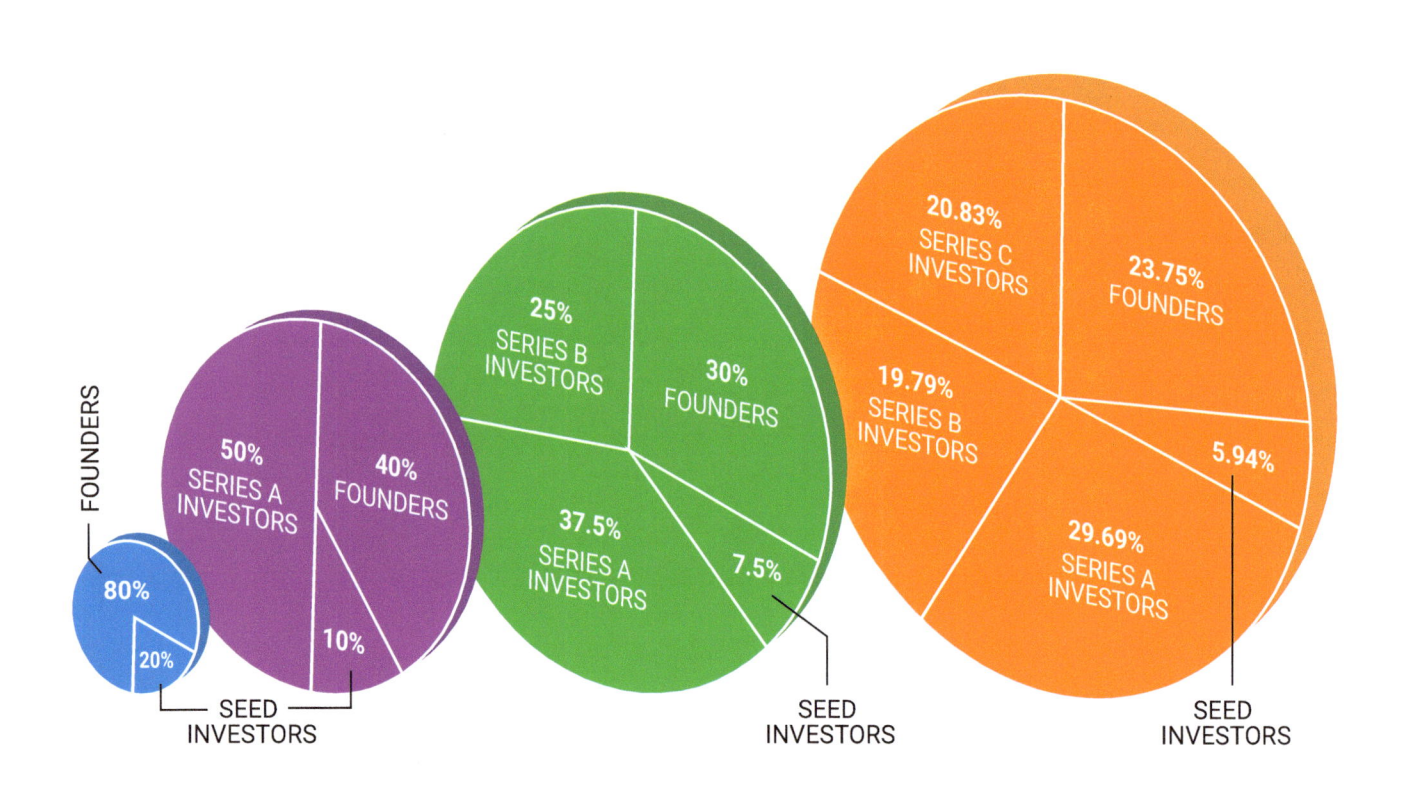

6.8: VALUATION AND FUNDING  44

Now, let's assume that the company is sold for $240M. Here are the net returns received:

|  | Initial Investment | Return | Return Rate |
|---|---|---|---|
| Founders |  | $57M |  |
| Seed Investors | $1M | $14.25M | 14.25X |
| Series A Investors | $10M | $71.25M | 7.125X |
| Series B Investors | $20M | $47.5M | 2.375X |
| Series C Investors | $20M | $50M | 2.5X |

A few caveats on this hypothetical example:

1. Investors will typically require to reserve a portion of stock ownership for the management team. The amount varies, but around 10% is reasonable, which will usually come from the equity of the founders and the seed funding investors.

2. The distribution of proceeds from the sale of the company does not account for liquidation preferences. These can be complex and dramatically change the distribution of the returns especially in favor of later investors.

3. Founders need to balance the preservation of ownership with attracting investment that will allow the company to achieve milestones that increase the overall company value. Remember that 100% of nothing is still nothing.

**The key takeaway of this example for startup founders is not to focus on the dilution but on the increase of value that each round of funding will bring.** In this example, the founders' stake increased from $4M pre-money valuation to $57M when the company was sold. It is common to see much lower percentages of ownership for founders than presented in this hypothetical example; this does not impede founders from obtaining very reasonable returns.

# SECTION 7
# CASE STUDIES

# CASE STUDY: SFC FLUIDICS

The goal of this case is to **illustrate the value of stakeholder interviews** in shaping the right market entry strategy. This study also illustrates the value of:

- Precisely defining the unmet need
- Defining the right product attributes
- Understanding the value of all stakeholders
- Partnering with advocates and foundations

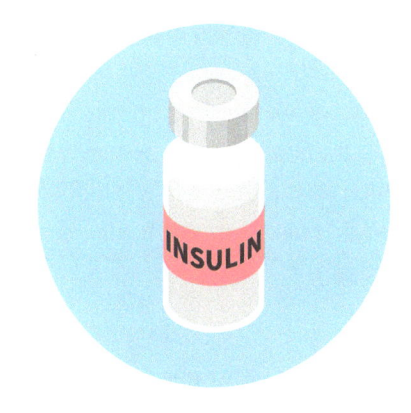

## Introduction

A university startup company was formed to develop and commercialize what they described as an artificial pancreas patch pump that can administer two different hormones and includes an instantaneous occlusion sensor. The medical problem they address is the growing diabetes epidemic and the need for effective blood glucose control. While there are current treatments involving insulin pumps, there is a high rate of noncompliance and low rate of adoption because the existing pumps are bulky, expensive, and may require multiple pumps for multiple drugs.

## Unmet Need Validation

The group embarked on stakeholder discovery and validation of an unmet need in the marketplace. They started by identifying the stakeholders that they considered critical and scheduled a number of interviews. They allocated three months to complete all the interviews and analyze the data. Their goal was to clearly define the unmet need, validate the key product attributes—those product benefits and features that stakeholders value most—and start relations with key opinion leaders (KOL)—endocrinologists, payors, funding sources, and advocacy groups.

| Stakeholders | # Interviews |
|---|---|
| Patients | 10 |
| Patient Family Members | 5 |
| Endocrinologists/KOL | 10 |
| Certified Diabetes Educators | 6 |
| Drug Companies (Diabetes/Glucagon) | 3 |
| Payors | 3 |
| Potential Partners/VCs | 2 |
| Advocacy Groups (JDRF) | 1 |

As a result of their interviews, the team learned that the products currently on the market and approved for type 1 diabetes patients are bulky, complicated, and include external tubing. What patients want is a miniaturized insulin delivery device that is easy to wear and includes open-protocol communication capabilities for compatibility. In other words, the unmet need was for a system that improves a patient's quality of life while keeping their glucose levels within range.

The stakeholders' interviews enabled the team to better define the key attributes of their product:

- Small patch pump
- Open communication protocol
- Bluetooth technology
- Interoperability with continuous glucose monitors and third-party algorithms

During the interviews, the company developed a great relationship with the Juvenile Diabetes Research Foundation (JDRF), which took great interest in their project and provided specifications for a product that they could fund. Some of the key attributes indicated above came from JDRF.

## Business Validation

During the interviews, the company also learned that they should initially focus on type 1 diabetes patients instead of all diabetes patients, as they do not produce insulin and do not have alternatives to control their blood sugar that many type 2 patients have. There are approximately 1.5 million type 1 diabetes patients in the USA and about the same number in Europe.

The team also discovered that there are reimbursement codes for a three-day patch that will cover the cost of their patch ($8) and leave a healthy margin for a sales price of $28. The total available market (TAM) for the U.S. is $4 billion. Assuming an adoption rate of 20 percent in five years, the serviceable available market (SAM) is $800 million.

The team found an **economically viable market fit.**

## Commercialization Risk

Challenges remained for the team. They needed to collect enough scientifically rigorous evidence to achieve regulatory and reimbursement approvals. They would also need to ensure adoption by the ordering clinicians, especially the certified diabetes educators.

The team assembled a Killer Experiment to confirm some of the technical requirements:

Stability of the hormones in the pump for five days based on FDA requirements for previously approved devices

- Biocompatibility using ISO 10993-1
- Integrated Bluetooth technology
- Interoperability protocol

**Regulatory**
During the interviews, the company discovered that they could meet the requirements of a simple patch pump that delivers insulin for three days in a shorter time frame than the full-blown artificial pancreas because it would only require 510(k) clearance instead of PMA. (During the next iteration of the product—a single-hormone artificial pancreas—they would apply for a PMA, which would take two additional years. Finally, they would seek approval for the dual-hormone artificial pancreas.)

**Marketing**
During the stakeholder interviews, they discovered that certified diabetes educators are critical for product adoption. These educators become the patient's trusted partner in managing their diabetes and a source of knowledge of all treatment advances. The company would need to invest heavily in training educators to understand the product utility. Of course, direct-to-patient marketing would be also necessary, as well as partnerships with patient advocacy groups and foundations.

## Where is the company in 2019?

- Hired a professional CEO
- Received an SBIR Phase 2 award of $1.4 million
- Received a two-year $3 million commitment from JDRF to accelerate development and regulatory submission

# CASE STUDY: VERACYTE

The goal of this case is to illustrate how the selection of the right medical problem for a specific technology is key for the success of a company. This selection is called **Market Fit.**

This study also illustrates the value of developing:

- A creative regulatory strategy
- A Killer Experiment design that answers the relevant clinical question
- Development of reimbursement competencies

## Introduction

In 2008, a group of researchers expert in sequencing technology hypothesized that they could develop a diagnostic test for liver cancer based on their current research. They formed a company, Veracyte, and garnered investment from a group of venture capital firms that recommended a talented CEO with deep expertise in the diagnostic industry. The CEO's first concern was that a screening test for liver cancer was not in high demand, as the incidence of liver cancer is less than 1 in 10,000 patients. Furthermore, a liver cancer test is a Class III product. The FDA would require a PMA, which would entail a screening test of the general population and be cost prohibitive.

## Unmet Need Validation

The group decided to explore more valuable uses for their technology. They interviewed more than 100 cancer clinicians and pathologists and spoke with other stakeholders, including hospital administrators and insurance companies. They reviewed all type of cancers, looking for the best market fit for their technology.

They found several possible candidates, and after an analysis of business viability and economic value, they settled on thyroid cancer, a slow-growing cancer type.

## Cycle of Care

The team traced the cycle of care for thyroid cancer. Thyroid nodules are detected during a regular checkup by a primary care doctor or by the endocrinologist for patients already diagnosed with thyroid problems. Once nodules are detected, patients are scheduled for a fine-needle aspiration (FNA) performed by a trained radiologist under local anesthesia and guided by ultrasound. The collected cells are sent to pathology, where the diagnosis is made. Endocrinologists reviewing the results decide whether patients need surgery.

## Business Validation

In the U.S., more than 525,000 patients each year undergo FNA biopsies to assess potentially cancerous thyroid nodules. Up to a third of these FNAs produce inconclusive results. Historically, most of these patients were directed to surgery to remove all or part of their thyroids for a more definitive diagnosis, but many of these nodules (70–80 percent) proved to be benign, meaning that surgery was unnecessary. Thyroid surgeries are invasive, expensive (~$20k), and potentially risky, and they often result in patients requiring lifelong daily thyroid hormone replacement therapy.

Vearcyte's diagnostic technology could reduce the number of unnecessary thyroid surgeries and spare patients a lifetime of unnecessary hormone therapy. They concluded that there was an unmet need that would benefit patients and certainly payors. The team did a quick business viability analysis:

- The total available market (TAM) = the 525,000 patients yearly who receive FNA biopsies

- The serviceable available market (SAM) = those patients who receive an inconclusive result (approximately 1/3 of the TAM)

- The serviceable obtainable market (SOM) = the portion of those inconclusive cases for which the new test would be recommended. Once the test becomes the standard of care, this would 150,000 – 175,000 cases. However, because market penetration requires education, the team deduced that they could achieve 50% penetration in 5 years, or about 80,000 patients. **Based on this number, the yearly savings to the health care system would be more than $1.5 billion in the U.S. alone.**

At $3,000 per test (equivalent to 15% of the cost of the surgery):

- SAM = $450 million
- SOM = $225 million

**The team found an economically viable market fit.**

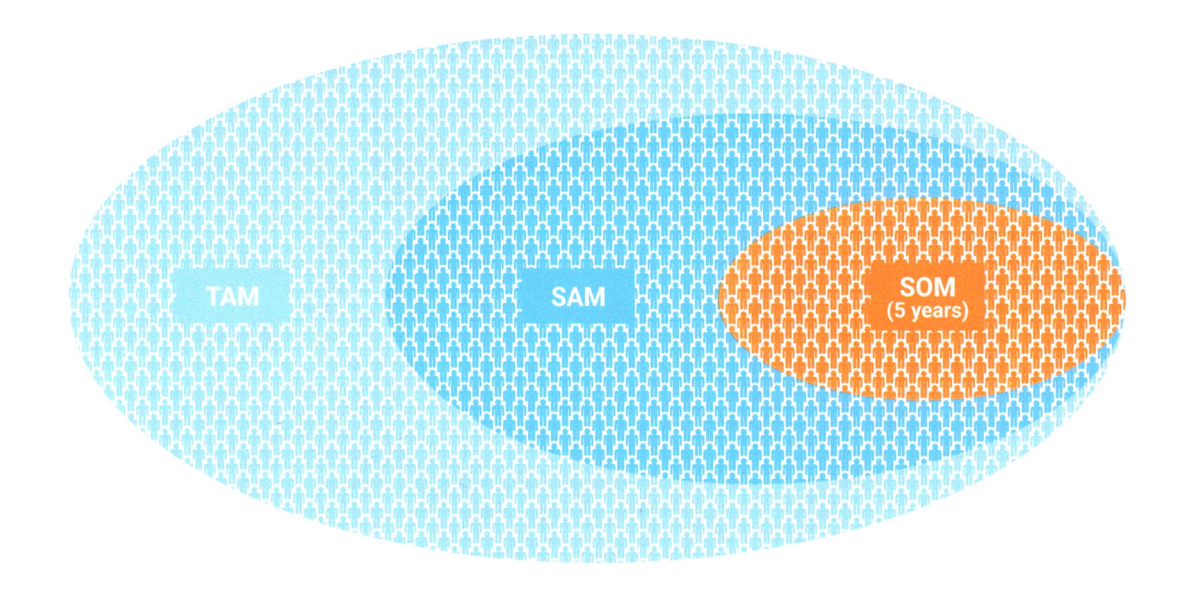

## Commercialization Risks

The Veracyte team knew that they could answer the right clinical question, but significant challenges remained. They needed to collect enough scientifically-rigorous evidence to achieve regulatory and reimbursement approvals. They also needed to ensure adoption by FNA-ordering clinicians, which would require education and sizable marketing efforts.

### Regulatory

The company's test translates complex genomic data into clinically meaningful information that changes patient care. It utilizes a proprietary machine learning algorithm to interpret vast genomic data using a large number of diverse patient samples that represent the broad spectrum of diseases the genomic test may encounter in a clinical setting. This complex test can only be performed by the company using their proprietary method; therefore, their regulatory strategy was to set up a CLIA* laboratory that will receive the patient samples, process them, and provide results to the originating clinician.

### Reimbursement

The success of the company's strategy hinged on getting payors to approve their price. To accomplish this, they designed and initiated clinical utility and cost-effectiveness studies early on so they could quickly demonstrate value to physician and payors. With robust clinical evidence, they focused on developing expertise in payor relations to gain policy coverage and in-network contracts, which facilitated test adoption and their desired level of reimbursement.

## Where is the company in 2019?

- Publicly traded
- Sales of $100 million/year
- 2018 sales growth rate 37% over 2017
- Market value over $700 million
- 300+ employees
- Two new tests introduced

---

*CLIA stands for Clinical Laboratory Improvement Amendments. The purpose of CLIA is to set minimum standards for all laboratories to follow and to determine whether laboratories are achieving those standards. Any person or facility that performs laboratory tests on human specimens for the purpose of diagnosis and/or treatment is required by federal law to have a CLIA certificate.

# CONCLUSION

We hope this guide has provided you with a helpful overview of the exciting but challenging road from lab to market. Each of these sections could be a lengthy manual in and of itself; we have done our best to highlight some of the key issues of which you should be aware. The health care market is ever-changing and sometimes frustrating but is of unparalleled importance not just to the economy but to society. We hope your innovation helps improve the lives of patients and efficacy of patient care and finds great success in the marketplace.

> Don't forget to visit the video library for supplemental resources. You'll find videos and presentations pertaining to every section of this guide.
>
> Visit www.biocomx.org/FLTM and enter the password c3i$Fltm

# APPENDIX

Sample Interview Guide

Sample Financial Statements

**SAMPLE INTERVIEW GUIDE**

**Questions for Catheter Design Inputs**

**Demographic info:**

Name: _____  Specialty: _____

Institution: _____  Institution Size (beds): _____

Monthly Procedure Volume: _____

Most common procedures performed: _____
_____

Highest complexity procedures: _____

**General Introduction:**
We are trying to better understand the selection criteria for catheters used in endovascular procedures. More specifically the challenges and limitations associated with more complex procedures.

1. As we understand it, there are different brands and types of catheters used in endovascular procedures.
    a. Do you typically start all procedures with the same catheter?
    b. Which brands(s) do you typically use?
    c. Are there particular ones that you use less frequently? Specialty? For which use?
    d. Does this preference vary between operators? Perhaps based on experience, training, or personal preference?

2. Do you select the specific catheters you will use <u>before the procedure</u>?
    a. Will this change your preferred catheters to start the procedure?
    b. Do you ever need to change the curvature of the catheters tip during the case?
    c. Do you change the size or type of the steerable catheters within a procedure?

3. What determines the specific catheter that you select for a given task?
    a. Does the specific procedure impact the initial catheters selection? How so?
    b. Does the anatomy you are targetting have an impact? Abdominal, head/neck, etc

4. What are some of the important attributes in considering particular steerable catheter?
    a. Durability - ability to work in more than one location with the same catheters
    b. Stiffness on the back end of the catheters?
    c. Ability to grip?

d. Tip properties?
   e. Others _____

5. What is the process to determine which catheters are stocked by your institution?

6. Does the complexity of the case impact the need for imaging?
   a. Is the total imaging time a concern for the patient or operator?
   b. Do you measure exposure time?
   c. Do you measure contrast agent use?

7. Are there particular goals or limitations for radiation and contrast use?

   **Introduce concept**
   We are working with a team that is developing an electronically steerable catheter. This steerable catheter will have the ability to articulate in any direction desired by turning knobs located at the proximal end of the catheters without the need for complex manipulation of common catheters.

8. Given this description, what are the potential advantages and disadvantages of such a product?

9. Are there specific concerns that come to mind?

10. Are there particular procedures that a product like this might be especially useful for? What would be the most desirable characteristics for the related steerable catheters (diameter, locations where it might articulate, length, etc.)?

11. What would it take to convince you to try/adopt a new steerable catheter?


Based on our discussion, are there any points that you would like to discuss?
Have we failed to consider anything?

# FINANCIAL STATEMENTS

## STATEMENT OF INCOME

| | |
|---|---:|
| **Revenues** | $ 1,000,000 |
| **Cost of goods sold** | 200,000 |
| Gross profit | 800,000 |
| **Operating expenses** | |
| Selling, general, and administrative expense | 357,700 |
| Interest expense | 20,000 |
| Depreciation and amortization expense | 5,200 |
| Operating income | 437,100 |
| Interest income | 20,000 |
| **Net earnings before taxes** | 437,100 |
| Income tax expense | 240,000 |
| **Net income** | $ 197,000 |

## STOCKHOLDER'S EQUITY

| | | |
|---|---:|---:|
| Beginning Balance | | $ X,XXX |
| Plus: | | |
| Stock Sales | $ X,XXX | |
| Net Income | X,XXX | |
| Subtotal | | X,XXX |
| Less: | X,XXX | |
| Dividends | X,XXX | |
| **Ending Balance** | | $ X,XXX |

## BALANCE SHEET

**ASSETS**

| | |
|---|---:|
| Cash | $ X,XXX |
| Accounts Receivable | X,XXX |
| Fixed Assets | X,XXX |
| Other Assets | X,XXX |
| Total Assets | X,XXX |

**LIABILITIES**

| | | |
|---|---:|---:|
| Accounts Payable | | X,XXX |
| Accrued Expenses | | X,XXX |
| Notes Payable | X,XXX | |
| Total Liabilities | | X,XXX |

**STOCKHOLDERS EQUITY**

| | |
|---|---:|
| Common Stock | X,XXX |
| Retained Earnings | X,XXX |
| **Total Liabilities and Stockholders' Equity** | X,XXX |

## STATEMENT OF CASH FLOWS

***Cash flows from Operating Activities***

| | |
|---|---:|
| Net Income | $ X,XXX |
| Plus: Depreciation | X,XXX |
| Adjustments to reconcile Net Income to Cash Flows from Operating Activities: | |
| Changes in Current Assets | X,XXX |
| Changes In Current Liabilities | X,XXX |
| Total Cash flows from Operating Activities | X,XXX |

***Cash flows from Investing Activities***

| | |
|---|---:|
| Purchase new PP&E | X,XXX |
| Cash flows from Investing Activities | X,XXX |

***Cash flows from Financing Activities***

| | |
|---|---:|
| Owner Investment | X,XXX |
| Owner Drawing | X,XXX |
| Total Cash flows from Financing Activities | X,XXX |
| Net Cash flows | X,XXX |
| Beginning Cash Balance | X,XXX |
| **Ending Cash Balance** | $ X,XXX |

CPSIA information can be obtained
at www.ICGtesting.com
Printed in the USA
LVHW072031131119
637244LV00003B/47/P